Calming Upset Customers

Stay in control... in any situation

Fourth Edition

Rebecca L. Morgan, CSP, CMC

A Crisp Fifty-Minute™ Series Book

AXZO PRESS

Calming Upset Customers

Stay in control… in any situation

Fourth Edition

Rebecca L. Morgan, CSP, CMC

CREDITS:

President, Axzo Press:	**Jon Winder**
Vice President, Product Development:	**Charles G. Blum**
Vice President, Operations:	**Josh Pincus**
Director, Publishing Systems Development:	**Dan Quackenbush**
Copy Editor:	**Catherine M. Albano**

ISBN 10: 1-4260-1834-7
ISBN 13: 978-1-4260-1834-3
Printed in the United States of America
2 3 4 5 6 7 8 9 10 13 12 11 10

Table of Contents

About the Author...1

Preface..2

About the Crisp 50-Minute Series 5

A Note to Instructors 6

Part 1: The Importance of Calming Upset Customers   **7**

Customer Satisfaction: Everyone's Job 9

Upset Customers Don't Come Back 10

You *Want* Customers to Complain 11

A Customer Is…..14

Assessing Yourself 15

Part Summary..18

Part 2: Why Customers Get Upset   **19**

Start by Looking for the Cause 21

Avoidable Upsets 23

Listening and Returning Calls...25

Part Summary..28

Part 3: Preventing Behaviors That Irritate Others   **29**

Personal Presentation 31

Nonverbal Communication 33

Words That Make a Difference 37

Part Summary..46

Part 4: Practicing Behaviors That Calm Customers   **47**

Take Action to Reverse Anger 49

Ten Steps for Dealing with an Upset Customer...................................54

Case Studies..56

After the Customer Has Gone 64

Part Summary..67

Part 5: Tips For Managers   **69**

Creating an Environment for Customer Satisfaction 71

Using this Book for a Staff Meeting 74

Calming Upset Customers and Employees...76

Part Summary..78

Appendix   79

Appendix to Part 3 81

Appendix to Part 4 83

Additional Reading 86

About the Author

Rebecca L. Morgan, CSP, CMC, is a workforce effectiveness expert. Since 1980, she's traveled internationally to help make people and organizations more productive and profitable. Her areas of expertise include sales, time management, communication, and creating customer service excellence. She is the author of eight popular books:

▶ *Professional Selling: Practical Secrets for Successful Sales*

▶ *Remarkable Customer Service… and Disservice*

▶ *Grow Your Key Talent*

▶ *TurboTime: Maximizing Your Results through Technology*

▶ *Life's Lessons: Insights and Information for a Richer Life*

▶ *Inspiring Others to Win*

▶ *Best Practices in Customer Service*

▶ *Calming Upset Customers*

Rebecca has produced numerous audio programs, special reports, and customer service manager discussion guides. She's been featured on and in hundreds of media, including the Oprah Winfrey Show, 60 Minutes, *Wall Street Journal*, *USA Today*, National Public Radio, *Home Office Computing*, and *Sales and Marketing Management* magazine. She has been a regular columnist for The Customer Communicator, and has had articles published in and/or been interviewed by *The Service Edge*, *First-Rate Customer Service*, *CRM Magazine*, and many others.

She's helped numerous companies create environments that delight customers. Her long-term solutions focus on profitability and attracting and retaining customers.

Rebecca has earned the designation of Certified Speaking Professional (CSP), which is conferred by the National Speakers Association (NSA). In 1993, when Rebecca received her CSP degree, only 214 people worldwide—less than 7% of the 3,200 NSA members—had earned this designation. She's also earned the Certified Management Consultant (CMC) designation, making her only the fifteenth person in the world to earn both designations.

Rebecca can be reached at:
Morgan Seminar Group
1440 Newport Avenue
San Jose, CA 95125-3329

Phone: 408-998-7977
Fax: 408-998-1742

www.RebeccaMorgan.com
rebecca@rebeccamorgan.com

Preface

Wouldn't it be wonderful if there were no upset customers to contend with? But that's not the way the world is. No matter how hard you try, you're bound to come across an upset person once in a while. You need to know how to respond quickly and professionally.

We have seen incidents of road rage, air rage, and general public anger escalate. C. Leslie Charles' popular book *Why Is Everyone So Cranky?* corroborates what we said in the very first edition of *Calming Upset Customers*—people are increasingly frustrated with everyday challenges, and often take out these frustrations on service personnel. This means that you have even more opportunity to hone your skills for calming upset customers! This book will help you develop those skills.

The Win/Win Solution

An article in *Nation's Business* quotes Doug Green, founder of New Hope Communications: "We've found that the solution to every problem comes from the spirit of cooperation. I am sure we can come up with something that can make both of us happy, but we must approach this in a very cooperative manner." This book will help you find those solutions.

"Upset" vs. "Difficult"

This book focuses on calming upset customers, who are different from *difficult* customers. When a reasonable person gets upset, she may have momentary lapses of unreasonableness, but she is still basically rational and reasonable. But difficult people have a psychological need to get attention by disruptive and negative means. They are chronically hard to communicate with.

Many of the ideas in this book will help you serve difficult people as well as upset people, but some people will be unreasonable no matter what you do. Sometimes you will have to call in your supervisor.

Customers Are Often a Challenge

You can learn from that challenge. The more you learn, the more you'll enjoy your job. Learning to calm upset people is not easy. There is no single technique that works with every upset person. But there are skills that can be learned, with a positive attitude and practice. By the way, the ideas and skills presented in this book also work at home.

Who Should Read This Book?

This book is designed to assist people who deal with the upset public to "keep their heads." The ideas presented here have been useful to people in retail, banking, insurance, medicine, utilities government, hospitality, travel, manufacturing, and other vocations. These ideas and techniques can be adapted to your job, your personal life, and your customers.

"Customers" in this book refers to clients, patients, passengers, ratepayers, insureds, taxpayers, homeowners, guests, students, patrons, or any other member of the public that you deal with who ultimately pays your salary. The concepts discussed are applicable to face-to-face interactions, telephone conversations, and even e-mail and letters.

This fourth edition of *Calming Upset Customers* includes updated information. As before, this book provides practical, easily adaptable ideas that will help you to deal effectively with upset customers in all types of situations.

Learning Objectives

Complete this book, and you'll know how to:

1) Understand the importance of upset customers to improving your business.

2) Identify common causes of customer's upsets, and learn why listening is a critical skill in dealing with them.

3) Be proactive in preventing upset customers.

4) Use various techniques to calm upset customers.

5) Practice management behaviors that calm upset customers and employees.

Workplace and Management Competencies mapping

For over 30 years, business and industry has utilized competency models to select employees. The trend to use competency-based approaches in education and training, assessment, and development of workers has experienced a more recent emergence within the Employment and Training Administration (ETA), a division of the United States Department of Labor.

The ETA's General Competency Model Framework spans a wide array of competencies from the more basic competencies, such as reading and writing, to more advanced occupation-specific competencies. The Crisp Series finds its home in what the ETA refers to as the Workplace Competencies and the Management Competencies.

Calming Upset Customers covers information vital to mastering the following competencies:

Workplace Competencies:

▶ Adaptability & Flexibility

▶ Customer Focus

▶ Problem Solving & Decision Making

Management Competencies:

▶ Supporting Others

▶ Managing Conflict & Team Building

For a comprehensive mapping of Crisp Series titles to the Workplace and Management competencies, visit www.CrispSeries.com.

About the Crisp 50-Minute Series

The Crisp 50-Minute Series was designed to cover critical business and professional development topics in the shortest possible time. Our easy-to-read, easy-to-understand format can be used for self-study or for classroom training. With a wealth of hands-on exercises, the 50-Minute books keep you engaged and help you retain critical skills.

What You Need to Know

We designed the Crisp 50-Minute Series to be as self-explanatory as possible. But there are a few things you should know before you begin the book.

Exercises

Exercises look like this:

EXERCISE TITLE

Questions and other information would be here.

Keep a pencil handy. Any time you see an exercise, you should try to complete it. If the exercise has specific answers, an answer key will be provided in the appendix. (Some exercises ask you to think about your own opinions or situation; these types of exercises will not have answer keys.)

Forms

A heading like this means that the rest of the page is a form:

FORMHEAD

Forms are meant to be reusable. You might want to make a photocopy of a form before you fill it out, so that you can use it again later.

A Note to Instructors

We've tried to make the Crisp 50-Minute Series books as useful as possible as classroom training manuals. Here are some of the features we provide for instructors:

▶ PowerPoint presentations

▶ Answer keys

▶ Assessments

▶ Customization

PowerPoint Presentations

You can download a PowerPoint presentation for this book from our Web site at www.CrispSeries.com.

Answer keys

If an exercise has specific answers, an answer key will be provided in the appendix. (Some exercises ask you to think about your own opinions or situation; these types of exercises will not have answer keys.)

Assessments

For each 50-Minute Series book, we have developed a 35- to 50-item assessment. The assessment for this book is available at www.CrispSeries.com. *Assessments should not be used in any employee-selection process.*

Customization

Crisp books can be quickly and easily customized to meet your needs—from adding your logo to developing proprietary content. Crisp books are available in print and electronic form. For more information on customization, see www.CrispSeries.com.

The Importance of Calming Upset Customers

If you can keep your head when all about you are losing theirs and blaming it on you… yours is the Earth and everything that's in it."

–Rudyard Kipling

In this part:

- ▶ Customer Satisfaction: Everyone's Job
- ▶ Upset Customers Don't Come Back
- ▶ You *Want* Customers to Complain
- ▶ A Customer Is…
- ▶ Assessing Yourself

Customer Satisfaction: Everyone's Job

The Financial Institution Marketing Association and the Raddon Financial Group conducted a survey of service quality. It reported that 25% of customers had expressed a complaint in the previous 12 months. The survey went on to state:

> "In light of this significant percentage, everyone in the organization—from teller to president—must become increasingly aware that he or she is either serving the customer directly or is serving someone in the organization who serves the customer. All positions exist because of the customer."

Calming upset customers is rarely enjoyable, but it must be done. If upset people continue expressing their anger and frustration without intervention, it can upset the whole office.

THE IMPORTANCE OF CALMING UPSET CUSTOMERS

Why do you feel it's important to calm upset customers?

_____

_____

_____

_____

_____

_____

Upset Customers Don't Come Back

A recent study by e-Satisfy (formerly the Technical Assistance Research Program, a top research company on customer service issues based in Arlington, VA) showed the following breakdown for customer dissatisfaction:

▶ 20% is caused by employee actions.

▶ 40% is caused by corporate products and processes that have an inherent and unwanted surprise for the customer.

▶ 40% are caused by customer mistakes or incorrect expectations.

Another survey showed that one out of every five supermarket customers had switched stores in the last 12 months. What made them switch? The way they were treated at the cash registers, mostly. People want and expect good service, and when they are not treated well, they don't come back.

It can be expensive for your company if your customers decide not to come back. Researchers at e-Satisfy found that the cost ratio between winning a new customer versus retaining a current customer varies from 2 to 1 to 20 to 1. That money could be spent improving your work environment, giving you a raise, or keeping you employed.

Word of Mouth Spreads Quickly

If your organization has a reputation for quick, courteous responses to complaints, people will be more apt to begin their conversation with you rationally. When customers scream and yell, it's often because that's what their friends had to do to get some action from your organization. One study found that, on average, one dissatisfied customer tells 11 other people, who each tells 5 others. That's 67 (1 + 11 + 55) people badmouthing your organization. Most organizations will be hurt by that much bad advertising.

A recent International Customer Service Association/e-Satisfy Benchmarking Study of Electronic Customer Service found that poor handling of online contacts created at least 30% lower customer loyalty among the two-thirds of online contacts who are not satisfied. Additionally, the study found that poor handling of online contacts resulted in a high level of negative word-of-mouth; dissatisfied online customers told twice as many people as satisfied customers (both online and offline) about their experience.

You *Want* Customers to Complain

Yes, you do. Because if they don't complain, you won't know there's a problem. They'll just take their business elsewhere, and tell their friends not to do business with you. Consider what happens when you are treated poorly: Do you usually complain? Many people don't. They just think, "I'm never coming here again."

A study conducted by e-Satisfy discovered that 96% of consumers do not complain to the retailer from whom they buy unsatisfactory items. This means that for every complaint the average business receives, there are possibly 24 silent unhappy customers.

Interestingly, e-Satisfy also found that on average, for large-ticket items, 50% of customers complain to frontline employees, and 50% of complainers escalate to local management or corporate heads. The existence of an 800 number at corporate headquarters will, on average, double the number of complaints at that level. However, only 1 out of 100–500 will actually be addressed to a senior executive. Complaint rates vary by type of problem. Problems that result in out-of-pocket monetary loss have high complaint rates (e.g., 50–75%), whereas mistreatment, quality, and incompetence problems result in only 5–30% complaint rates.

In addition, e-Satisfy found that customers who complain and are subsequently satisfied are up to 8% more loyal than if they had never had a problem at all.

Therefore, if a customer does complain, he or she is more likely to come back. The act of complaining can actually increase customer loyalty.

Unhappy Customer Return Rates*	
No complaint:	9% (91% won't come back)
Complaint not resolved:	19% (81% won't come back)
Complaint resolved:	54% (46% won't come back)
Complaint resolved quickly:	82% (18% won't come back)
*Percentage of customers with major cause for complaint (over $100 losses) who will buy from you again.	

Source: U.S. OCA/White House National Consumer Survey

In a study reported in the Yankelovich Monitor, 54% of adults agreed with the following statement: "It is usually a waste of time to complain to a big company when you're not satisfied with a product or service."

Another study by Yankelovich Partners revealed that 90% of customers say they feel they pay enough to get the highest level of service. Yet, 64% say the service representatives they deal with don't care about their needs.

So remember: Encourage customers to complain when they have a problem. And then do something to help resolve the matter!

WHAT I CAN LEARN FROM UPSET CUSTOMERS

We can learn from every experience, if we choose to do so. A difficult encounter can be an opportunity to learn something new, or to apply what you've learned. What can you learn from dealing with upset customers?

I can learn:

_____

_____

_____

_____

_____

_____

What You Can Learn

Recall your worst encounter with an upset customer. You don't ever want to complain like that. Isn't anger ugly when expressed inappropriately? If you practice the following, you will succeed at preventing and calming anger in others.

- ▶ Have patience. It takes a lot of patience to listen attentively to someone while they are yelling.

- ▶ Identify specific organization procedures or practices that may be annoying to your customers. Then you can work to change these.

- ▶ Improve yourself. There may be something in your behavior that irritates people. You can work at changing this.

- ▶ Show confidence. People can tell when you are confident in your skills. An irate person is more apt to hassle someone who appears unsure of himself.

- ▶ Learn how to calm upset people. Practice your calming skills.

Richard Bach, in his book, *Illusions*, wrote: "You are never given a problem without a gift for you in its hand." We are given gifts in these upset people.

CALMING UPSET CUSTOMERS IN YOUR WORKPLACE

We looked at why it is important to calm upset customers, and to actually solicit complaints from unhappy customers. Now apply these ideas to your work situation.

Why is it important for *you* to calm upset customers?

_____

_____

_____

_____

Why is it important for you to encourage unhappy customers to complain?

_____

_____

_____

_____

_____

A Customer Is…

▶ The most important person to come into my organization, whether in person, on the phone, or by fax, email, or mail.

▶ The person who ultimately pays my salary. I really work for her.

▶ Not someone with whom I should argue. Dale Carnegie said, "The only way to get the best of an argument is to avoid it"—especially with customers.

▶ Someone with whom I will learn patience, although he is not always patient with me.

▶ Someone who can make or break my day, depending upon how I react to comments. I can easily control my life by controlling how I respond to situations.

▶ Someone who has biases and prejudices just like I do. He may not like my hair; I may not like his clothes. Yet he is a special human being and my customer.

▶ Someone I take care not to offend. Even when she is wrong, I point out the mistake indirectly and politely.

▶ Sometimes a challenge. I embrace the challenge and am glad when I can turn a frown into a smile.

▶ Very special. She is my customer for a few short minutes and I focus on serving her needs 100% when I am helping her.

▶ Someone for whom I will go the "extra mile." He may not realize it, but I realize that the difference between mediocre and excellent is just 10%.

"Now THIS is my idea of a happening Customer Lounge."

Assessing Yourself

MY SKILLS AT CALMING UPSET CUSTOMERS

Write the number of the your response in the blank to the left of each statement, using the 1 to 5 scale below.

1 = Never   2 = Rarely   3 = Sometimes   4 = Usually   5 = Always

_____ 1. I feel I can calm most upset customers.

When I'm with an upset customer, I:

_____ 2. Stay calm.

_____ 3. Don't interrupt.

_____ 4. Focus on his/her concern without getting distracted.

_____ 5. Respond to personal accusations without becoming defensive.

_____ 6. Reduce distractions of paperwork and telephone.

_____ 7. Have attentive body posture.

_____ 8. Have appropriate facial expressions.

_____ 9. Have confident eye contact.

_____ 10. Listen completely before responding.

_____ 11. Take notes when appropriate.

_____ 12. Show empathy.

_____ 13. Let him/her know I want to help.

_____ **TOTAL**

Scoring

81–100: Excellent.
61-80: Good.
41-60: You need to hone your skills.
21-40: You may need to ask your supervisor for help.
1-20: Start working with this book right now!

To make sure you have a realistic view of your skills, photocopy the following assessment and ask your boss or co-workers to complete it, based on their observations of how you work with upset customers. If their answers are very different from yours, discuss their evaluation with them.

CALMING SKILLS ASSESSMENT

I'm interested in being the best I can be. Please candidly assess my skills in calming upset customers, so I can know where to focus my efforts to improve.

1 = Never   2 = Rarely   3 = Sometimes   4 = Usually   5 = Always

_____ 1. (Name) _____ can calm most upset customers.

When a customer is upset, I believe that (name) _____:

_____ 2. Stays calm.

_____ 3. Doesn't interrupt.

_____ 4. Focuses on concern without getting distracted.

_____ 5. Responds to personal accusations without becoming defensive.

_____ 6. Reduces distractions of paperwork and telephone.

_____ 7. Has attentive body posture.

_____ 8. Has appropriate facial expressions.

_____ 9. Has confident eye contact.

_____ 10. Listens completely before responding.

_____ 11. Takes notes when appropriate.

_____ 12. Shows empathy.

_____ 13. Lets the customer know he/she wants to help.

CONTINUED

1 = Never   2 = Rarely   3 = Sometimes   4 = Usually   5 = Always

When a customer is upset, I believe that (name) _____:

____   14. Knows when to call on a supervisor.

____   15. Has a confident, helpful tone of voice.

____   16. Uses words that don't escalate the customer's anger.

____   17. Avoids blaming fellow workers or the organization for causing the problem.

After the upset customer leaves, (name) _____:

____   18. Is in control of his/her emotions.

____   19. Doesn't repeat the story more than once.

____   20. Analyzes what was done well and what needs to be done differently.

Suggestions to help (name) _____ become better with upset customers:

_____

_____

_____

_____

_____

Part Summary

In this part, you learned that customer satisfaction is **everyone's job**. You learned that **word of mouth** spreads quickly and that unhappy customers **don't come back**. Next, you learned the value of having **customers complain**, and what **you can learn** to deal with upset customers. You learned that **a customer is** a person who is important to you and your organization. Finally, you learned how to **assess** your own skill at calming upset customers.

Why Customers Get Upset

There is only one boss: the customer. And he can fire everybody in the company from the chairman on down, simply by spending his money somewhere else."

–Sam Walton

In this part:

▶ Start by Looking for the Cause

▶ Avoidable Upsets

▶ Listening and Returning Calls

Start by Looking for the Cause

Customers become upset for various reasons. Sometimes their anger is justified; sometimes it's not. Either way, in working to resolve their upset, it helps to know the cause.

WHY DO CUSTOMERS GET UPSET?

Why do you think customers get upset? Write three to five responses in the space provided, and then compare your answers with the list of reasons that follows this exercise.

1. He was already upset at someone or something
2. She feels that no one will listen to her unless she yells.
3. He will use any excuse to prove he's right.
4. He was told one thing by one staff member
5. She acted on something told her by a staff member and it was wrong.

A customer could be upset for any of the following reasons. It could be that the customer:

▶ Has expectations that have not been met

▶ Was already upset at someone or something else (his boss, his spouse, his kids, a co-worker, or other business)

▶ Is tired, stressed, or frustrated

▶ Feels like a victim—not much power in his life in general

▶ Believes that no one will listen to her unless she yells and makes a ruckus

▶ Wants an excuse to prove he is right, whether he is or not

▶ Walks around with a chip on her shoulder—nothing is right in her life

▶ Was treated rudely or indifferently by you or someone in your organization

▶ Has been told one thing by one staff member and something else by another

▶ Acted on something told to her by a staff member and it was wrong

▶ Feels you or someone else in your organization had an unpleasant attitude toward him

- Doesn't feel she was listened to

- Has prejudices—doesn't like your hair, clothes, voice, and so on

- Feels she can manipulate you to get what she wants by making a lot of noise

- Suspects you or your organization are dishonest

- Made a wrong assumption about what your organization would do

- Was told he has no right to be angry

- Was given a smart or flip reply

- Was transferred on the phone without consent, or was forced to sit on hold

- Was screened on the telephone

- Became embarrassed about doing something incorrectly

- Felt her integrity or honesty has been questioned

- Believes you or someone in your organization argued with him

- Decided don't have enough job training to handle the situation quickly and accurately.

Studies suggest that the causes of customer complaints can be attributed to one of three areas: individual employees, the company, or the customer, with 80% of complaints traceable to the last two categories.

Upset People Have Little Patience

Annoyances that a person can usually tolerate become intolerable when that individual is upset. You can't control another person's behavior. You can, however, change your behavior to avoid causing annoyance. Look again at the reasons why customers get upset. Which ones do you have any control over? In the space below, list those you think you can at least partially control, and briefly note what your responsibility is:

Causes I May Be Able to Control	Action I Can Take to Help
When I havebe emotionally comfortable	can I do something happy

Avoidable Upsets

You and your organization might bear some responsibility for annoying customers. The reasons might include any of the following:

▶ *You or someone in your organization promised something that was not delivered.*

If you promised the customer you would get back to him and you didn't, then he may become upset—with good reason. Most of us become upset when people promise action and don't follow through.

▶ *You or someone in your organization was indifferent, rude, or discourteous.*

Discourtesy is often unintentional. You may not have thought about your statement before you blurted it out. Some people try to make funny comments, but these may come across as rude. Treat every customer as you would a special guest or relative.

▶ *The customer feels you or someone else in your organization displayed an unpleasant attitude toward him.*

Perhaps this customer was surly himself, dressed unusually, or treated you poorly. Try to react professionally to all customers at all times.

Straighten Up and Fly Right!

While I was waiting in the airline check-in line, the ticket agent announced, "The line in front of me is for passengers checking in for Flight 64. The line to the right is for the problems."

▶ *She doesn't feel she was listened to.*

People want to be listened to. They don't want to have to repeat themselves. We'll go into this in more detail later.

▶ *He was told he had no right to be angry.*

Everyone has a right to his or her emotions. Telling a person otherwise is sure to make him or her even angrier.

▶ *She was given a smart or flip reply.*

Sarcastic remarks only heighten anger; they seldom ease it.

▶ *He is embarrassed about doing something incorrectly.*

Make sure the customer understands what he needs to know before he tries to use your product or service. Go over any procedures about returns or guarantees beforehand. That way, you'll have fewer customers who are angry because of a misunderstanding.

▶ *Her integrity or honesty has been questioned.*

Treat customers with respect and dignity. If there is a problem, assume your organization made the mistake. Instead of saying, "You didn't pay us," say, "We don't have a record of receiving your payment. Would you be kind enough to see if your check has cleared the bank?"

Work to eliminate body language, voice tone, or facial expressions that convey distrust. Avoid projecting an "us versus them" attitude to customers.

Never call a customer a deadbeat, liar, thief, and so on. Never threaten a customer.

Angel of Mercy

At 5:00 the nurse called my name. As she showed me to the examination room, I commented, "The doctor must be very busy today. I arrived at 4:05 for my 4:10 appointment." She responded, "I checked the waiting room for patients an hour ago. You must have been late for your appointment."

▶ *You or someone in your organization argued with the customer.*

As Dale Carnegie said: "The only way to get the best of an argument is to avoid it." This is especially true with customers. If you argue with a customer, you *always* lose—even if you win the argument. It's not good for other customers to witness an argument. They won't like seeing you treat a customer poorly, even if that customer was in the wrong.

"How about this for our motto: 'If you are unhappy, we will feel bad'?"

Listening and Returning Calls

Customers get upset when they are not listened to. One of the biggest causes of upset is when a customer doesn't feel the customer service provider listened to them. It's more common than any of us would like to admit.

SELF-REFLECTION: BEING LISTENED TO

Think about a time when you had to ask a customer to repeat what she had said. Why didn't you listen as well as you'd have liked? What habits do you think prevent people from listening fully, especially in stressful situations?

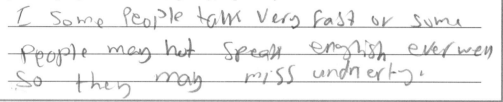

I Some People talk very fast or some People may not speak english ever wen so they may miss undnerty.

There can be many reasons we don't listen as well as we'd like. Some of them are beyond our control: a noisy environment or a customer who speaks softly or with an accent. But some of the reasons are within our control: distractions, trying to do two things at once, feeling we've heard the issue many times before, boredom, emotional triggers. We can definitely do something about these issues.

According to Dr. Lyman Steil, president of consulting firm Communication Development Inc., most people have poor listening habits. Some habits Dr. Steil discovered include the following:

▶ *Criticizing the speaker and delivery*

This focuses not on what the speaker is saying, but how she is saying it. If you focus on a lisp, a stutter, an accent, a dialect, grammatical errors, and "ums" and "uhs," you are missing the speaker's thoughts and feelings.

▶ *Listening only for facts and not for feelings*

A customer may not say he's angry, but his voice conveys it loudly and clearly. Listen carefully for emotions as well as facts.

▶ *Not taking notes—or trying to write everything down*

Not taking notes can cause problems later, when you try to remember what was said. On the other hand, trying to take down everything the customer says will make you lose eye contact. Take a few brief notes of important details, such as dates, times, amounts, and account numbers.

▶ *Faking attention*

Customers can quickly discern if you are paying attention to them or not. If a customer was mildly agitated before, your inattention will make her angry. Pay close attention when you are helping her.

▶ *Tolerating or creating distractions*

Don't be distracted by other conversations. Eliminate visual distractions by removing paper piles and pulling out a clean piece of paper to take notes. Listen fully to the customer and eliminate whatever distractions you can.

▶ *Tuning out difficult or confusing information*

When people are upset, they don't always communicate clearly. If you habitually tune out what you don't immediately understand, practice asking the person, in a pleasant manner, to slow down or repeat. It's easier to understand information one piece at a time. Take notes to help you put the pieces together.

▶ *Letting emotional words block the message*

The upset customer may call you names, curse, or say unpleasant things about you, your co-workers, and your organization. Avoid letting him "push your buttons" in this way, because when you're upset you've lost objectivity, and you need to be in control if you're going to find a solution to the situation.

▶ *Interrupting or finishing the other person's sentences*

This is an irritating habit and will only induce more anger in an already upset person.

▶ *Biases and prejudices*

We all have biases and prejudices, whether we like it or not. You may not like a person's style of dress, hairstyle, or stutter. It is hard to listen when you're distracted by these biases. Work on eliminating your prejudices to be a better listener.

▶ *Not facing the upset person*

Look her in the eye. Remember what your parents said when you were a kid: "Look at me when I'm talking to you." People see you are listening when you are looking at them.

▶ *Not ensuring that you've understood*

Repeat what you understand the customer to be saying. Start your sentence with, "Let's see if I understand…" or "I think I understand…" (and then paraphrase what she said). Don't say "What you're trying to say is…"—it implies the customer is an idiot and can't say what he means. Also avoid "What I hear you saying is…"—it's overused and trite.

Returning Calls

Following up with information you promised is one way you can avoid upsetting callers or visitors. Even if you have to call back to say you're still checking, she'll appreciate knowing that you haven't forgotten and are doing your best.

Below is a simple form you can duplicate to keep track of the follow-up responses you promise. If you have customers in different time zones, this will help you remember to call them back during their workday. Keep this form in front of you to remind you of what you've promised.

CALLBACK SCHEDULER

Call	Name	Phone	Regarding
before 8:00			
before 9:00			
before 10:00			
before 11:00			
before 12:00			
before 1:00			
before 2:00			
before 3:00			
before 4:00			
before 5:00			

Part Summary

In this part, you began by looking for the cause of customer upsets. Then, you learned that some upsets are avoidable, and reviewed some sample causes. Finally, you learned the value of listening and of returning calls.

Preventing
Behaviors That
Irritate Others

If the shopper feels like it was poor service, then it was poor service. We are in the customer perception business."

–Mark Perrault, Rally Stores

In this part:

- ▶ Personal Presentation
- ▶ Nonverbal Communication
- ▶ Words That Make a Difference

Personal Presentation

We will now look at what you can do to avoid turning a dissatisfied customer into an angry one. By being proactive in how you present yourself to customers, you can directly influence whether a minor irritation escalates into an angry confrontation.

One of the things that can irritate an already upset customer is your personal presentation. If he feels your grooming and dress are unprofessional or inappropriate, he is more likely to hassle you.

Here are some areas of personal presentation that, if not seen to, may have a negative influence on an upset person. Check to make sure that your:

▶ Hair is clean, brushed or combed, and well kept.

▶ Makeup is applied neatly, moderately, and appropriately.

▶ Clothing is pressed, neat, clean, and in good repair.

▶ Hands and fingernails are clean.

▶ Nail polish is fresh and unchipped.

▶ Face is shaved or mustache/beard is trimmed neatly.

▶ Stockings are run-free.

▶ Breath is fresh.

CHECKING PERSONAL PRESENTATION

Can you think of anything other than the items in the preceding list that you should check about your personal presentation?

Well an make assessment of others, and initially those assessment are based on Personal Presentation

How can your personal presentation affect how an upset customer reacts to you?

Some experts we make decisions about people within the first seenes of meeting them.

First Impressions

We all make assessments of others, and initially those assessments are based on personal presentation. Some experts claim we make decisions about people within the first 4 seconds of meeting them.

> **If you are in a position where you are likely to interact with angry customers, you have a chance to use your image as one of your more effective tools. You can use your image to signal your power, control, knowledge, and composure. If you are dressed inappropriately or too casually for your position and business, customers are more likely to push to get their way, and call for a higher authority if they don't like your response."**
>
> **–Bay Alexander, President of Professional Impact**

You may have experienced the power of your appearance when you were a customer. Have you noticed how much easier it is to return an item to a store when you are neatly dressed than when you wear torn jeans and an old T-shirt?

You never get a second chance to make a good first impression.

Nonverbal Communication

Here are some ways body language and voice tone may influence an upset person:

- ▶ Facial expression
- ▶ Body posture
- ▶ Movement
- ▶ Gestures
- ▶ Smoking
- ▶ Touching
- ▶ Chewing gum or eating
- ▶ Voice tone
- ▶ Sighing
- ▶ Cursing

Facial Expression

When people complain, do you ever roll your eyes? Do you scowl? Do you have an inappropriate smile?

Be aware of your facial expression when you communicate. Ask friends, co-workers, and your supervisor whether you have facial expressions that could be annoying, especially to upset customers.

You want to have a calm, concerned, sincere, interested facial expression. Show the customer you care.

Some people smile when they are tense; don't smile when a customer is expressing anger. If you do, the customer may feel that you're not taking her seriously.

Body Posture

Do you loll about your work area? Do you slouch?

Show you are attentive to your customer by standing and sitting up straight. When you loll or slouch you may seem inattentive or disinterested.

Maintain a nonthreatening, open body posture. Stand far enough away to give the customer room. Don't crowd him—this may increase his irritation.

Movement

Do you move slowly when you have to find something for the upset customer?

Upset customers want to see you respond to their needs quickly. This doesn't mean you have to sprint to help, but don't take your time either.

Gestures

Do you stand or sit with arms crossed? Do you rest your head on your hand?

The most common interpretation of the arms-crossed gesture is that the person is closed and unwilling to listen. When communicating with an upset customer, uncross your arms to show you are listening and have an open mind.

Smoking

Don't smoke in front of customers, even if your employer allows you to smoke in your work area. Always put the cigarette out, even if your customer is smoking.

Touching

Avoid touching an upset person, especially if he appears potentially violent. Touching also implies familiarity and is inappropriate with customers, upset or not.

Chewing Gum or Eating

Don't chew gum or eat when you're on the phone or in the public eye. Even if your employer allows it, these acts can be annoying, and can change an upset customer into an irate one.

Voice Tone

Your attitude is projected through your voice. Remember that helping customers is your job, and if you can't stand to help upset people, get transferred to another job. Make sure your attitude is always, "I'm here to help as best I can."

Do you sound annoyed? Does your voice go up at the end of a statement?

People respond more strongly to how you say something than to what you say. When your voice is annoyed, impatient, or condescending, the customer will become angrier. When your voice sounds confident, she will believe you know what you're talking about and it will be easier to calm her.

When your voice goes up at the end of a sentence, it sounds as if you're asking a question. Record and listen to your voice and note whether your voice goes up at the end. If so, practice having an even tone, or one that ends on a lower note. You will sound confident and competent.

Speak with a calm, firm, caring, and soothing tone.

Sighing

Sighing often suggests annoyance or impatience. Don't sigh in front of an upset customer.

Cursing

Even if the customer curses, there is never an excuse for you to curse. No matter how many insults he shouts at you, remember that you are a professional. Compose yourself as best you can and avoid responding to abuse.

It is a sign of strength, not weakness, to stay calm and respond with patience when someone is cursing and insulting you.

"I'm Mario, your Master of Intimidation for the evening."

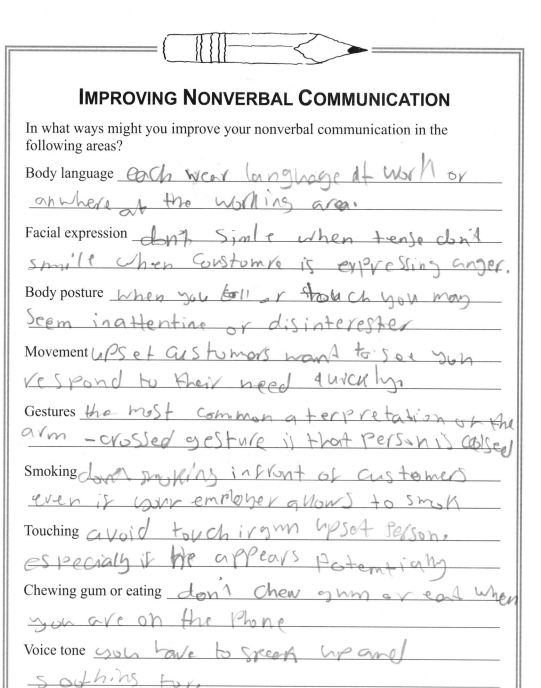

IMPROVING NONVERBAL COMMUNICATION

In what ways might you improve your nonverbal communication in the following areas?

Body language _each wear langhage at work or anwhere at the working area._

Facial expression _don't simle when tense don't smile when custromre is expressing anger._

Body posture _when you toll or touch you may seem inattentine or disinterester_

Movement _upset custumors want to see you respond to their need quickly._

Gestures _the most common a terpretation of the arm-crossed gesture is that person is closed_

Smoking _don't smoking infront of customers even if your employer allows to smok_

Touching _avoid touch irgm upset person, especialy if he appears potentially_

Chewing gum or eating _don't chew gum or eat when you are on the phone_

Voice tone _you have to speeak up and sothing tori_

Sighing _do not sing infront of the customer_

Words That Make a Difference

The words you use with customers can help communicate or they can start a disagreement. Here are some common Fight Starters and some suggestions for replacing them with Communication Helpers:

▶ Keep it impersonal

▶ Use *I* instead of *you*

▶ Avoid giving orders

▶ Take responsibility

▶ Avoid causing defensiveness

▶ Use verbal cushions—show empathy

▶ Use the three Fs: feel, felt, found

▶ Get clarification

▶ Form a team

Keep It Impersonal

Fight Starter	Communication Helper
You didn't do this right.	*There are a few areas on this form that we need to complete.*

If the customer did something wrong, point out the mistake indirectly. She will often be embarrassed by her mistake. She may get angry because of this embarrassment and try to blame you.

Avoid statements that are sarcastic, blaming, or condescending. Even if the customer is wrong, the time to make it known is not during a rage.

Use *I* Instead of *You*

Fight Starter	Communication Helper
You're wrong.	*I can see there's been a miscommunication (or misunderstanding).*
Fight Starter	**Communication Helper**
You're confusing me.	*I'm confused.*

Don't blame the customer. When explaining what went wrong, use either the indirect approach or *I* statements as much as possible.

Avoid Giving Orders

Fight Starter	Communication Helper
You have to…	*Can I ask you to please…?*
you are not the nest	*It would be best if we…*
I'm not the best	*It would be best if you…*

People like to be given a choice. Ask them pleasantly to do something or explain how it will be to their benefit

People don't like to be given orders. Rephrase it more politely as a question.

Fight Starter	Communication Helper
You should have done it this way.	*We want your next visit to go as smoothly as possible. This will assist you.*
Fight Starter	**Communication Helper**
Wait here.	*Would you mind waiting while I speak to my supervisor?*

When people hear "should," they often think of their parents or some other authority figure telling them what they did wrong. It also implies that it is the customer's responsibility to learn how your system works.

Instead of telling them what they should have done, tell them what will be helpful in the future. The past is past and there's nothing anyone can do about it. Focus on the future—the next time—instead.

Take Responsibility

Tell the customer what he and you can do—not what can't be done.

Fight Starter	Communication Helper
I can't... help you with omything but I may get help you lete	*I don't have that authority. However, Mary should be able to help you. Let me get her.* *You can...*

If you cannot help, connect the customer with someone who can.

Fight Starter	Communication Helper
It's not my job. how way you first day at work	*Let me see what I can do to help.* *John is the specialist in that area. Let me get him to help us.*

Even if what the customer needs isn't within your job duties, never tell her that. Tell her how you can help.

If people think they're being criticized, they'll react defensively—that is, angrily.

Avoid Causing Defensiveness

Try to avoid using words that will put a listener on the defensive. Accusations or suggestions that the listener is at fault will tend to make them defensive. They will stop listening to your words while they mentally arm themselves for battle.

Fight Starter	Communication Helper
You never do it right.	*This is often not done correctly.*
You're always late.	*This payment is often late.*

"Always" and "never" sound critical and uncompromising; use "often" instead.

Fight Starter	Communication Helper
You filled this out okay, but...	*You filled this out well, and...*

People don't listen to what you say before the "but"; they concentrate on what follows. Use "and" instead, so they'll listen to the whole sentence.

Fight Starter	Communication Helper
It will cost you...	*The rate for that is...*

"Cost" sounds negative, and costs can imply time, aggravation, and other things in addition to money.

Fight Starter	Communication Helper
What's your problem?	*Please tell me what happened.*

People don't like to have problems, and they don't like others to know they have problems. Use the communication helper instead.

Here are some more words to avoid—because they'll enrage someone who's already irritated—and alternatives that help to defuse their upset.

Use Verbal Cushions—Show Empathy

Verbal cushions let the customer know that you can understand why she would be upset. You're not saying you know exactly how she feels, because you can't know that.

You're also acknowledging her right to feel that way. You're not discounting her feelings.

Fight Starters	Communication Helpers
You're crazy.	*I can appreciate what you're saying.*
I know how you feel.	*I can understand how you'd feel that way.* *I can understand how that would be annoying.*
Boy, you're sure mad.	*I can see how you'd be upset.*
I don't know why you're so upset.	*I'm sorry for your inconvenience.*

Use the Three Fs: Feel, Felt, Found

The three Fs are a frame on which to hang the rest of your response. This technique acknowledges the customer's feelings and offers an explanation in a way she can listen to:

"I understand how you could feel that way. Others have felt that way too. And then they found, after an explanation, that this policy protected them, so it made sense."

Get Clarification

Paraphrase what is said. Take the blame if there is a miscommunication. Make sure you understand the concern before you try to solve it.

Fight Starters	Communication Helpers
You're way off base.	*I'm sorry. I need to better understand...*
You aren't making any sense.	*Maybe I misunderstood...*
That's definitely wrong.	*Let me see if I've got this straight...*
Did you really say...?	*Here's what I understood you to say...*

Form a Team

Let her know her patronage is important. When you form a team, it is the two of you together working on a solution, rather than her versus you.

Fight Starters	Communication Helpers
We can't do that.	*I want to help find a solution.*
You sure have a problem.	*Let's see what we can work out together.*

WATCH YOUR WORDS

How would you respond in the following situations?

Customer: *Can you put this sweater on hold for me?*
Staff: *I can only hold it until closing.*

1. Why wouldn't you say this to a customer? _because they may not comeback for it,_

How would you rephrase the response? _sure, no problem but try your best to show up before closing_

Customer: *I would like to be on the preferred customer mailing list.*
Staff: *You have to have spent $1,000 or more.*

2. Why wouldn't you say this to a customer? _Because they might not have this much & then wont come back._

How would you rephrase the response? _I would like to but let me try & see if you can._

Customer: *Why haven't I received my refund?*
Staff: *Because you filled in the form wrong.*

3. Why wouldn't you say this to a customer? _because they might get angry & leave._

How would you rephrase the response? _maybe something happened wrong, let me check again._

Customer: *Do you have mittens?*
Staff: *You'll have to go to accessories for that.*

4. Why wouldn't you say this to a customer? _because they may not come back to store again._

How would you rephrase the response? _I'm sorry we don't carry them but you can try the accessories_

CONTINUED

> **Customer:** *Are there any more of these forms?*
> **Staff:** *I don't think so.*

5. Why wouldn't you say this to a customer? *because they will think you don't like to help them*

How would you rephrase the response? *I am not sure but let me check for you*

> **Customer:** *How can I reach Dr. Jackson?*
> **Staff:** *Call her.*

6. Why wouldn't you say this to a customer? *because wouldn't so say this.*

How would you rephrase the response? *I will see how can you reach her? give you the code*

> **Customer:** *I'd like to change something on that job you're doing for me.*
> **Staff:** *You'll have to come to our office tomorrow. It's too late today.*

7. Why wouldn't you say this to a customer? *because they might not be able to show up tomorrow.*

How would you rephrase the response? *Sure how can I help to change it.*

> **Customer:** *Why can't I get my software to run?*
> **Staff:** *Because you didn't read the manual.*

8. Why wouldn't you say this to a customer? *Because they would think you mean they are stupid.*

How would you rephrase the response? *Let's try again together maybe something want wrong.*

Customer: *I need the number for one of your branch offices.*
Staff: *I'm busy with a customer. Here, you can look it up.*

9. Why wouldn't you say this to a customer? _The Customer_
will get mad.

How would you rephrase the response? _just give me a_
second I ll give it to you

Customer: *I got a refund for $24.95 when I requested $42.59.*
Staff: *You must have sent in the request for $24.95; otherwise, we would have sent you the other amount.*

10. Why wouldn't you say this to a customer? _because must_
have requested & get mean

How would you rephrase the response? _may be they get_
messed up with number let me take
care of it for you.

Customer: *How do I get to the Shamrock Room?*
Staff: *There's a map over there.*

11. Why wouldn't you say this to a customer? _Because might_
not know how to use map

How would you rephrase the response? _let me walk_
you there.

Customer: *Why haven't I received my order yet?*
Staff: *Because I've been handling customer problems.*

12. Why wouldn't you say this to a customer? _because they will_
Feel they're less important.

How would you rephrase the response? _I am really sorry_
I ll check if there was any problem during
ordering.

Customer: *Why do I need to show ID? I've banked here for years.*
Staff: *It's bank policy.*

13. Why wouldn't you say this to a customer? *because its*
bank Policy

How would you rephrase the response? *It's for security*

_____

Customer: *I need someone to help me with a problem on my account.*
Staff: *You'll have to wait for Susan to get back from lunch.*

14. Why wouldn't you say this to a customer? *because he might*
not be able to stay untill

How would you rephrase the response? *I'll see how San*
I hep you.

Customer: *How do I make this computer I bought from you run?*
Staff: *It's in the manual.*

15. Why wouldn't you say this to a customer? *He/She will*
feel they are not important to be

How would you rephrase the response? *I'll write* haped
down the steps for you.

Customer: *Would you check the status on our account?*
Staff: *The computer is down. You'll have to call back tomorrow.*

16. Why wouldn't you say this to a customer? *because a customer*
might get upset & transfer to another bank.

How would you rephrase the response? *I would like to*
help you but hope you can come later.

Compare your responses with those of the author in the Appendix.

Part Summary

In this part, you learned how to use your **personal presentation** to avoid having a negative impact on an upset person. Then, you learned how **nonverbal communication** such as body language and voice tone may influence an upset customer. Finally, you learned that **words make a difference**. You learned how to substitute **Communication Helpers** for potential **Fight Starters**.

Practicing Behaviors That Calm Customers

Customers don't expect you to be perfect. They do expect you to fix things when they go wrong."

–Donald Porter, V.P., British Airways

In this part:

▶ Take Action to Reverse Anger

▶ Ten Steps for Dealing with an Upset Customer

▶ Case Studies

▶ After the Customer Has Gone

Take Action to Reverse Anger

We've discussed how your personal presentation, body language, voice tone, and choice of words can irritate customers. Once the customer is angry—for whatever reason—you need techniques for calming him down. In this section, we'll look at:

▶ What upset customers want

▶ Additional pointers

▶ Calming customers over the phone

▶ Calming customers via e-mail

Then, we'll talk about the steps you can take when dealing with an upset customer.

What the Customer Wants

Your customer wants:

▶ **To be taken seriously**

The customer does not want a response like "You're kidding," "No way," or "You've got to be joking." He wants you to be professional and confident and to respond seriously to his concern.

▶ **To be treated with respect**

The upset person doesn't want condescension or arrogance. She wants you to treat her and her concern with respect. This may be difficult when the customer is clearly at fault but is trying to blame your organization.

▶ **Immediate action**

He doesn't want you to look into it next month, next week, or even tomorrow. He wants you to do something now. Show you are concerned by moving briskly, no matter how tired you are.

▶ **Compensation/restitution**

She wants someone to pay for the damage done, and perhaps for her time, inconvenience, or pain.

▶ **Someone to be reprimanded and/or punished**

Assure the customer that corrective action will be taken, even if you aren't the supervisor. Discreetly report the incident to the supervisor so he can explain the problem to your co-worker and prevent similar problems in the future.

▶ **To clear up the problem so that it never happens again**

Sometimes the customer just wants to know that some action has been put in motion, so that no one will have this problem again. Assure her you will report the problem to the person who can take care of it.

▶ **To be listened to**

What the upset customer wants first is to be listened to. It is difficult to listen carefully in a tense situation, especially if you have not developed effective listening habits. (For an excellent book on listening skills, read the Crisp Series' *The Business of Listening* by Diana Bonet.)

Additional Pointers

Take Time Out

If you find yourself becoming upset, or wanting to cry or yell at the customer, allow yourself a little time away from the situation. This will give you a chance to calm down before you address the problem.

When you know you're getting emotional, excuse yourself politely:

> *Excuse me a moment while I check the policy on this.*

> *I'd like to get my supervisor's opinion on this.*

> *I need to verify some information in the file.*

> *I need to discuss how we can best solve this. I'll be just a moment.*

Always excuse yourself in a way that shows your interest in serving the customer.

Don't Cry

Upset customers can say things that are hurtful, often without realizing that you may take comments personally. Whatever you do, don't cry in front of the customer. If your emotions take over, you cannot be as professional as you need to be.

If you find yourself beginning to cry, excuse yourself and go to an empty office, the rest room, or a back room so you can compose yourself undisturbed. If you don't feel you can bear talking with the customer, ask one of your colleagues or your boss to take over.

Get the Customer's Attention

If the customer is ranting and not giving you a chance to explain or ask questions, use his or her name at the beginning of your sentence. Most people listen when they hear their name.

Handle the Obstinate Customer

If you are having trouble reaching an agreement, make comments that direct the customer toward finding a solution:

What would you like me to do now?

What do you think is a fair way to settle this?

What would make you happy?

Often, what she will ask for is less than you might have offered. If the customer's proposal is within your guidelines, accept it. If not, make a counterproposal.

If you can't reach an agreement, it's time to call in your boss. Unless you are a manager, it is not your place to invite a customer to take her business elsewhere.

Use Polite Repetition

If the customer keeps insisting on something that's unreasonable or impossible, tell them what you can do (not what you can't do). Keep repeating it, without becoming hostile or loud, until you're finally heard. For example, if the customer insists on getting a widget, and you have none in stock, the conversation might go like this:

Customer: *I want my widget today.*

You: *I'm sorry; we'll have more widgets in on Thursday.*

Customer: *But I need it today!*

You: *I'm sorry; we don't have any in stock.*

Customer: *I want it today.*

You: *I'll be glad to get one to you on Thursday.*

If you cannot prevail, offer to refer the customer to your supervisor.

A Special Note on Dealing with Violence

There may be occasions when an enraged customer threatens you, or becomes violent. Rely on your gut feeling if it seems things are getting out of hand. Learn to look for potentially violent behavior by reading the nonverbal communication of the customer—clenched fists, tight lips, agitated tone of voice, tense body posture, flared nostrils, red face, and wide-open eyes. Look for evidence of drugs or alcohol.

If the customer becomes unruly, or threatens violence, seek assistance. You do not have to put up with threats.

Never try to reason with a drunk or a drug user. Even if there is no sign of drugs, if the person appears potentially violent, don't feel stupid about calling the police. There are plenty of stories about employees being struck by upset customers. It's better to risk feeling stupid than to end up in the hospital.

Never accuse a customer of being drunk or on drugs—this can be the beginning of a lawsuit. Find another way to assist the customer away from your establishment. For more information, read the Crisp Series book *Preventing Workplace Violence* by Marianne Minor.

Calming Customers over the Phone

It is easier for a customer to be abusive on the phone because you are a faceless representation of the organization. The guidelines we've discussed throughout this book generally apply when calming customers on the phone. There are a few areas you'll need to modify, however.

Because there is no face-to-face contact, communicating over the phone presents special challenges. You only have your voice tone (e.g., inflection, pitch, and volume) and word choice to communicate your caring to the customer.

You can see how critical it is that your voice tone be pleasant, concerned, patient, informed, and caring. When a customer cannot see your concerned face, she needs to hear concern in your voice. It also helps to deepen your telephone voice. Lower voices are perceived as being more mature, confident, and in control.

There are several ways to check whether you have a good voice tone. One way is to get feedback from your boss or a co-worker. It must be someone who will be honest with you, yet offer feedback caringly. Another option is to record yourself. Although your recorded voice may sound different to you than you think it should, this is an excellent way to discover how others hear you.

You could still be annoying customers, even if your voice is pleasant. You may have irritating habits, such as mumbling, gum chewing, eating, covering the receiver to talk to co-workers, or leaving the customer on hold too long.

If you need to leave the line during a call, ask the customer if she'd rather be called back or put on hold. If she prefers to be called back, tell her you'll call her by a certain time, and ask if that's acceptable. Call back at the agreed time, even if you've nothing to report except that you're still working on the problem.

If she prefers to be kept on hold, explain that it may be several minutes before you'll have the information. Give her your name and telephone extension in case she decides to hang up and needs to call again. And ask for her number in case you get disconnected.

This kind of service shows the customer that she really matters, and that your organization is run by thoughtful, helpful people, not cold computers.

Calming Customers via E-mail

Just as calming an upset customer on the phone has special considerations, so does calming a customer via e-mail. It is easy to misinterpret words, tone, and intent in an e-mail. You must be extra careful to word your e-mail response to an upset customer, so your message doesn't further irritate the customer.

▶ Create boilerplate responses to the most common issues addressed via e-mail. Work with your supervisor to word these carefully so that they are friendly, and prevent the possibility of misinterpretation. However, make sure your response fits the customer's question or concern. It can be doubly annoying to receive a form response that doesn't address the question asked.

▶ Be friendly in your word choice, but not too casual.

▶ Because e-mail messages cannot convey facial expression or tone of voice, humor rarely works in a tense situation. Sarcasm almost always fails, and can make a bad situation worse.

▶ Check your message thoroughly for typos.

▶ Thank the customer for letting your organization know there is a problem, and outline your steps for rectifying it.

▶ Show concern for the customer's situation and frustration.

▶ State any additional information you need from the customer.

▶ Give the customer your direct telephone number in case she wants to talk to a live person.

▶ If you have technical notes pertaining to the inquiry, copy the text into your response, rather than just referring the customer to a Web page.

Ten Steps for Dealing with an Upset Customer

When you're dealing with an upset customer:

1 Verbally cushion the customer's concerns.

"I can understand how that would be frustrating."

"The manual can be confusing."

2 Use the three Fs.

"I can understand how you could feel that way. I felt that way when I first heard our policy. So I asked my supervisor, and found out how it really protects our customers. Let me share what I learned…"

3 Apologize for the situation.

"I'm sorry that no one has called you about this."

"I apologize for your inconvenience."

4 State that you want to help.

"I want to find a solution for this situation."

"I want to resolve this for you as quickly as possible."

5 Probe for more information.

"Help me understand more…"

"Please tell me what happened."

6 Repeat the concern to make sure you have understood.

"Let me see if I understand correctly…"

"Before proceeding, I want to make sure I have all the facts right…"

7 Show that you value the customer's patronage.

"We value your business and want to fix this promptly for you."

"You are an important customer so we want to resolve this quickly for you."

8 **Explain options or ask what the customer would like to have happen.**

"There are three different actions I can take to resolve this. Which would you prefer?"

"What do you think would be a fair way to resolve this?"

9 **Summarize actions to be taken—yours and the customer's.**

"Mr. Garcia, as we agreed, you'll fax me a copy of the notice you received, and I'll take it immediately to my manager for resolution."

10 **End pleasantly.**

"Ms. Fukumoto, I'm sorry this has been a hassle for you. I appreciate your bringing this to our attention so we can straighten it out immediately. Thank you for calling."

Throughout:

▶ Listen.

▶ Face the customer.

▶ Look him/her in the eye.

▶ Adopt a concerned body posture, voice tone, and facial expression.

▶ Avoid Fight Starters.

▶ Avoid a condescending or impatient tone.

▶ Have and show empathy.

▶ Eliminate distractions.

▶ Practice patience.

▶ Use a pleasant tone of voice.

▶ Don't take things personally.

Case Studies

Case studies provide insights you may not gain by just reading about ideas and skills. Case studies present specific situations to think about and to show how you can apply important ideas and skills to real situations. These cases do not have exact solutions or answers. Different points of view are always possible—and even encouraged—in discussions of people, their attitudes, and their behaviors. You can benefit from these case studies by doing two things:

▶ Analyze the case and express your views.

▶ Compare your ideas with the author's comments in the Appendix.

CASE STUDY: The Surly Salesperson

Salespeople can inadvertently cause an upset by the way they approach customers. That was the case in the following conversation, a portion of an actual call from a national long-distance phone company sales representative.

Salesperson: "I'm with [name]. I'm calling about your video, Calming Upset Customers. Why don't you use an 800 number?"

Rebecca: "We do use one. Say, where did you hear about the video?"

Salesperson: "I have an ad you placed in a magazine."

Rebecca: "Hmm. I didn't place an ad. What magazine is it in?"

Salesperson: "I don't know. I'll ask my supervisor. (At this point, he turns away without covering the phone or putting the potential customer on hold, and asks supervisor.) She thinks it was a telemarketing magazine."

Rebecca: "Oh, it was probably the press release in Inbound/Outbound."

Salesperson: "So, why don't you have an 800 number?"

Rebecca: "(Struggling to continue to be polite) As I told you, we do."

Salesperson: "Well, it's not through our company."

Rebecca: "You're right. We researched 800 numbers last summer and were told we couldn't get one from you on our type of line."

Salesperson: "That's not right. Who told you that?"

Rebecca: "One of your representatives, six months ago."

Salesperson: "Well, it wasn't me. So why isn't your 800 number in the ad?"

Rebecca: "(Almost losing patience) Because we didn't *place* an ad... "

CONTINUED

■ CONTINUED ■

What did this salesperson do wrong? What should he have done differently?

_____

_____

_____

_____

_____

_____

_____

_____

Compare your responses with those of the author in the appendix.

"Sizzling… smoking… flames shooting from the hard drive.
OK… that *is* a malfunction and you'd best unplug it."

CASE STUDY: The Annoying Airline Agents

Suzanne arrived at the airline counter of a small regional airport to check in for the last flight of the evening to a small town called Kearney. It took 4 or 5 minutes for the young agent to help the two people ahead of Suzanne. Now it's Suzanne's turn. The agent busily begins typing into the computer.

Suzanne, after waiting a few minutes more: "It says 'check-in required' on my ticket."

Agent 1 (without looking up): "The other agent will be right with you," nodding toward another agent (Agent 2).

Agent 2 steps to Suzanne's left to ask a colleague something. Another passenger approaches him and he spends a few minutes helping him. The agent then turns to his computer to complete a task. Another passenger interrupts him.

Suzanne: "Excuse me," she says, beginning to get impatient, "I was next."

Agent 2: "I'll be with you in a moment, ma'am."

Suzanne: "I was next and you've already waited on two people who weren't in line."

Agent 2: "I'll be right there."

Suzanne is beginning to fume.

Agent 2: "Please be patient. This is our first day."

Suzanne: "Great," she says sarcastically. "Let me share a little phrase that will help you a lot. It's 'Who was next?'"

Agent 2 now gives her a boarding pass. They don't say another word.

Suzanne's flight is announced. Agent 1 is collecting tickets, while chatting with another airline employee. Suzanne doesn't see anyone else boarding for the flight; maybe she's the only one going to this small town. There are three doors leading to the tarmac. None have flight numbers or destinations posted near them. She proceeds down the hallway toward the one she thought was her flight. She walks out into the darkness and proceeds down the flight of stairs to the tarmac. The nearest plane is dark—no lights in the cabin, and no one onboard. A pilot and another airline employee stand nearby.

CONTINUED

"Is this the plane to Kearney?" Suzanne asks, confused because the plane is dark.

"No," the employee answers, "You'll have to go back and ask the agent where the plane is."

Suzanne is now furious about the confusion and the airline's unresponsiveness. She meets another airline employee in the hallway. "Where's the plane to Kearney?" she seethes.

"It's down the other hallway," she says, motioning with her head.

"That agent is an incompetent twit," Suzanne hisses.

"No she's not. You shouldn't say that about her," the employee retorts.

What did each of the airline employees do wrong? How could they have handled the situation more positively?

_____
_____
_____
_____
_____
_____
_____
_____
_____
_____
_____

Compare your responses to those of the author in the Appendix.

CASE STUDY: The Flighty Travel Agent

Robert calls a national travel agency he's been using and asks for the manager. When he gets the manager, the conversation proceeds as follows:

Robert: "Hello, I've had several problems getting the right ticket for a flight I'm leaving on tomorrow. I need someone who will take some responsibility."

Manager: "What's the problem?"

Robert: "Six weeks ago Tomas sent me a ticket, but it had the wrong date. I called immediately and was told by Bianca not to worry. I would be reticketed closer to my travel date."

Manager: "Bianca no longer works here."

Robert: "Yes, I was told that today when I called. Tomas quoted me a $99 fare, but the ticket showed $329, and Bianca said it should be $279. She promised to send new tickets on Friday. When I didn't receive them on Monday, I called again. Your office told me to call the Miami service center, so I did. There Louisa said a supervisor would call me that day, Monday. No one did. Today is Wednesday. I'm supposed to leave tomorrow."

Manager: "When did you notice the problem?"

Robert: "Six weeks ago."

Manager: "And you're just now getting around to calling about it?"

What did the manager do wrong? How should he have handled the situation?

_____

_____

_____

_____

_____

_____

_____

_____

_____

Compare your responses with those of the author in the Appendix.

CASE STUDY: The Nervy Newsman

The sales rep of a local weekly business journal calls Bill, a customer. Here's part of the conversation:

Salesperson: "Do you plan to resubscribe?"

Bill: "No, I don't."

Salesperson: "Why not?"

Bill: "Well, I decided the paper just wasn't worth $42 a year to me."

Salesperson: "Are you kidding? What are you looking for that we don't have?"

Bill: "I get more business information out of the daily paper."

Salesperson: "I can't believe that. We have better business coverage than they do."

Bill: "That's subjective."

Salesperson: "No, it's not!"

What did this salesperson do wrong? What should he have done differently?

_____

_____

_____

_____

_____

_____

_____

_____

_____

_____

Compare your responses with those of the author in the Appendix.

HOW WOULD YOU HANDLE THE SITUATION?

Here are some situations you might encounter in your organization. They won't be an exact match of your circumstances, but they may be similar.

Write your responses in dialogue form—what you would actually say, not a description of the scene. Then ask a co-worker to role-play these scenes with you aloud and give each other feedback.

Example:

Customer: "You have sent me someone else's canceled checks again. I have had it. I want to close my account right now."

Bank Teller: "I'm sorry about the mistake and I understand your frustration. If you'll give me your account number, I'll get you the correct checks immediately. We'd hate to lose you as a customer."

Now write your responses to the following complaints:

1. "I've waited in line for 20 minutes. What takes you people so long?"

_____

_____

_____

2. "You made a mistake again on my bill. My records say I owe $62.00 and your statement says I owe $323.50. I want you to fix it. Can't you people do anything right?"

_____

_____

_____

3. "Your service has been totally unsatisfactory. You promised to deliver my software three weeks ago and I haven't heard from anyone since. I want it delivered today."

_____

_____

_____

CONTINUED

4. "You have done this completely wrong. You are incompetent. I want to see your supervisor immediately so I can have you fired."

_____

_____

_____

5. "Your manager has been letting me do it this way for years. Even though she isn't in today, why don't you just let me do it this way so I can stop wasting my time here?"

_____

_____

_____

6. Write a scenario that has happened to you that you felt uneasy dealing with. Write the customer's part as well as your own. Describe how you would respond now, after reading this book.

How you would you have responded in the past?

_____

_____

_____

_____

_____

_____

How you would respond today?

_____

_____

_____

_____

_____

_____

_____

Compare your answers with those of the author in the Appendix.

After the Customer Has Gone

After the customer has left, you may want to take a few minutes for a time-out to cool down. You may need to compose and calm yourself.

Don't focus on what you did poorly. Don't reproach yourself for making mistakes. Instead, use this time to decide how you could handle the situation differently in the future. On the next page is an Incident Review form you can photocopy to review what happened.

INCIDENT REVIEW

1. What did I do well to calm this upset customer (for example, called the customer by name, looked the customer in the eye, listened well, wanted to help, avoided interrupting)?

   _____

   _____

2. What could I have said that would have calmed the customer better or sooner?

   _____

   _____

3. What did I say that I don't want to say again?

   _____

   _____

4. What body language can I use to calm the upset customer better next time?

   _____

   _____

5. What body language do I want to work on eliminating so it doesn't escalate the upset?

   _____

   _____

6. What did I learn?

   _____

   _____

7. Think of two phrases that will help you remember both your value and your intentions. Two examples include the following:

   ▷ I am a valuable person.

   ▷ I am working on becoming the best I can be.

   _____

   _____

Don't Take It Personally

Even though the customer is actually upset at the organization, a policy, one of your co-workers, or himself, it is easy to feel as if the attack was personal. The customer is lashing out at whatever is near—in this case, you.

More often than not, his misfortune was not caused by you. You must remind yourself of this. If he says "You screwed up my order," he probably means "My order didn't arrive on time and you people are going to pay for this. Whoever did this is in big trouble, and since I don't know exactly who it is, you're going to hear my anger—perhaps you'll put things right."

Sometimes the mistake was your fault. We all make mistakes. It often disarms people if you admit it was your fault and apologize. But only do this if it really was your fault. If you have made the same mistake before, ask your supervisor how you can eliminate the error.

Don't Bore Your Co-workers

Some people say it helps to get over their own upset if they tell their co-workers about the incident. Ask yourself, "Was this a pleasant experience?" If not, why would you want to share an unpleasant experience with people you like? Will it make their day better? Will it make them happier? The answer is no, it won't make their day happier, so why burden them?

If there is something your co-workers can learn from your experience, then certainly you should share it. For example, you may have learned something about a customer's hot buttons, because you unknowingly set them off. This information is useful to your co-workers, so they won't get into the same hassle with this customer.

You may also want to ask your co-worker for advice. "What would you have done?" "What do you think I should have done?" "What should I do differently next time?" These questions can help you learn from the experience.

If you just want to get it off your chest, however, don't bother anyone else. Write out the story to yourself. This way, you can become your own advisor. Ask yourself what you could have done differently.

Part Summary

In this part, you learned how to take action to **reverse anger** by giving customers **what they want**, calming customers **over the phone**, and calming customers **via e-mail**. Next, you learned **ten steps** for managing an upset customer. Then, you used **case studies** and **exercises** to role-play dealing with upset customers. Finally, you learned what to do—and what not to do—**after the customer leaves**.

Tips For Managers

"Your most unhappy customers are your greatest source of learning."

–Bill Gates

In this part:

▶ Creating an Environment for Customer Satisfaction

▶ Using This Book for a Staff Meeting

▶ Calming Upset Customers and Employees

Creating an Environment for Customer Satisfaction

Managers don't always know how customers are being treated. When you aren't around or within earshot, how do you really know how your employees are responding to your customers? You don't. Therefore, ensure that your example of customer service lives on through your staff's interactions with customers.

Some customers wouldn't have to be calmed were they not faced with annoyances to begin with. It is critical that you instill successful customer service concepts in your staff. Let's examine what managers can do to create an environment conducive to continual customer satisfaction.

Here are several ways in which you as a manager can create an environment that fosters customer satisfaction:

▶ Be a role model.

▶ Ask for your staff's suggestions.

▶ Solicit customer feedback.

▶ Reward good customer service behavior.

▶ Encourage your staff to use their initiative.

▶ Don't talk negatively about others.

▶ Know when to fire a customer.

Be a Role Model

You must give more than lip service to the concept of customer satisfaction—you must practice it visibly and frequently. Sending your staff to outside courses on customer satisfaction will be a waste of money if you don't model and reward good service.

Ask for Your Staff's Suggestions

Your employees often have good ideas to improve operations. However, some won't feel comfortable making suggestions unless asked.

Enact any ideas that make sense. Moreover, give credit for them. People resent it when someone else steals their thunder.

Solicit Customer Feedback

You have several inexpensive ways to get feedback:

▶ **Provide postage-paid return cards or surveys.**

Make sure they're short and to the point. Include a place for the customer to write his or her name and telephone number so you can call to clarify any information.

▶ **Follow up with phone calls.**

You could personally call 5 or 10 customers each week to check on service. Don't call only customers known to love your company, but also some from whom you haven't heard in a while.

Observe service interactions and ask customers what changes they'd like to see.

Reward Good Customer Service Behavior

When a staff member does a good job, give her immediate feedback. Let her know what you noticed that showed good service. Be specific: "I was glad to hear you offer Mrs. Olsen help with her packages."

Become familiar with the concepts in this book so you can reinforce behavior that calms customers, and counsel your staff when they are behaving in ways that are annoying to customers.

Encourage Your Staff to Use Initiative

Give your staff the authority to act on the customer's behalf. Set a guideline for how much money they can spend to resolve an issue without calling in a supervisor. Increase the amount as your trust in their judgment increases. This gives them confidence, and allows the customer's problem to be handled immediately.

In a recent article in *Frequent Flyer,* Paul Auger, vice-president of marketing for an airline, says:

"Employees now have the ability to resolve problems—whatever the problem is—without saying that our policy is 'Write a letter to the president.' For example, we tell our personnel we're not going to punish them for giving away a free ticket. We counsel them if we feel they're being overzealous. But as long as they feel they're doing it on behalf of the customer, the worst that can happen is that we say, 'Gee, did you really have to go that far?'"

Don't Speak Negatively about Others

You might think that saying "Mrs. Hanson is such a pain in the neck," teaches nothing. But in fact it does teach your employees that you don't respect Mrs. Hanson or value her business. If you don't, why should they? Instead, you could say, "Mrs. Hanson is very detail-oriented, so make sure to check her invoices carefully before you send them out," explains your concern and what to do about it.

Know When to Fire a Customer

If a customer continually upsets your staff for trivial reasons, you may need to invite the customer to use someone else's services. "Mr. Pratt, it seems that we cannot meet your expectations. Perhaps another vendor could meet your standards." Of course, if your organization is a utility, public agency, or government office, this is not an option for you.

"This is a photo of my blood pressure reading,
after dealing with your customer service."

Using this Book for a Staff Meeting

Using this workbook in a staff meeting can help to interest your staff in learning techniques for dealing with customers.

Hand out the books a week or two before your next staff meeting, telling everyone that the topic of the next meeting will be how to calm upset customers.

Make each employee responsible for reading the book, completing the exercises, and coming up with ideas on how to adapt the concepts to your group's unique circumstances.

When you lead the meeting, become a facilitator, not a dictator. Draw out your staff by asking them open-ended questions about the situations and concepts. Avoid lecturing. Although you are the boss, you will turn everyone off if you tell them that the way you handle people is the only right way.

Some questions you can use to begin the discussion include the following:

▶ *"Suzanne, share with us your response to question 4 of the 'Watch Your Words' practice, page 14, in Part 3. Would you elaborate on why you think it's important never to treat a customer the way the staff did in this example?"*

▶ *"Blake, how do you think we could adapt _____ here?"*

▶ *"What ideas do you have for eliminating things that could annoy our customers?"*

Have regular discussions at staff meetings about customer service. Provide examples of good customer service behavior, as well as problems that may need correcting. (Don't embarrass anyone.) Continually make your concerns and attitude known.

Teach Your Staff How to Learn From Negative Experiences

Use the questions in the Incident Review form:

▶ What did you do well?

▶ What would you do differently next time?

▶ What could you do to prevent this from happening again?

▶ What did you learn?

Evaluate Customer Satisfaction Performance

Be clear about the minimum levels of customer service you expect. Be specific. For example:

▶ Telephones to be answered within two rings

▶ All walk-in visitors greeted within 30 seconds

▶ Phone calls returned within four hours

▶ Upbeat and helpful behavior

▶ Smile when greeting customers

Let staff members know that their behavior in these areas will be included in their performance evaluation.

Calming Upset Customers and Employees

Calming Upset Customers

The upset customer may be passed to you if your employee can't handle the situation, or if the customer insists on seeing you.

Not only is there an urgent need to calm this customer, your staff are also listening and watching to see how you handle the situation. Remember that you are a role model.

Often, the customer will seem calmer and more rational with you than with your staff because you are perceived as having more authority to do something about the problem.

On the other hand, your staff may have done something to escalate the customer's anger. You should be able to handle any situation if you use the guidelines in this book.

When You Blow It

If you do or say something that annoys the customer further, and you realize your error in retrospect, see that as an opportunity for a teachable moment. Discuss it at a staff meeting. Explain what you did wrong, and either ask the group to suggest a better response or explain what you think you should have said or done.

A leader who is willing to admit errors, discuss them, and strategize corrections is a leader who will be respected. Don't be afraid of being vulnerable in front of your staff. If you talk about your mistakes and act to correct them, you will have the respect of your employees.

Managing Upset Employees

In addition to stepping in when necessary to calm upset customers yourself, one of your management responsibilities is to help employees through these experiences. At times, you may need to stand up for the employee and support him during an incident. You should also support the employee afterward, helping him regain composure and reclaim a positive footing. You can help your entire staff learn from each incident and provide a safe environment for learning from one another.

Part 1: During the Incident

Whether she's right or wrong, it's important that you not make your employee look foolish or incompetent.

If she was right in what she told the customer, say so.

> *"Mrs. Wong, I'm sorry to tell you that your Blue Bird phone service allows you to receive discounts only on calls made inside your area code between noon and 2 P.M. As Nancy explained, this is the reason the calls at 2:08 and 3:32 were charged at the full rate."*

If only you can make an exception to the policy your employee quoted, tell the customer so. Emphasize that the employee was doing her job well.

If the employee was wrong, explain that there must have been a misinterpretation of policy. Emphasize his value in front of the customer.

> *"Yes, Mr. Jones, you are right that you shouldn't be charged for cashiers' checks on your Senior Special account. Obviously, there was a misunderstanding about this. Bill is one of our finest tellers, so I'm sure it was an oversight. At our next staff meeting, I'll remind all our tellers. I'm sorry for your inconvenience. Of course, we'll waive the fee for your cashier's check. Is there anything else we can do for you today?"*

Part 2: After the Customer Has Left

Your employee may be shaken, angry, or on the verge of tears. Allow him or her to retain self-respect and composure in front of peers and the other customers. Give the employee a 10-minute break to go to the lounge, restroom, or other quiet place to regain composure.

If at all possible, accompany the employee and talk about the exchange. Listen to vented anger and reinforce your support of actions taken. When the employee is calm enough, discuss possible ways to handle the situation differently next time. (If the employee is very upset, postpone the discussion until another time.) Solicit ideas before offering yours. The last thing needed right now is a lecture.

Part 3: Debriefing the Rest of the Staff

If the rest of the staff heard or saw the incident, it may be appropriate to discuss the scene with them. If it was a serious or physical altercation, debrief them as soon as possible, preferably at the close of that business day or shift. If it was less serious, discuss it at the next staff meeting. Be sure to discuss it with the involved employee beforehand, and confirm that sharing this with others will be okay.

Recap what happened and focus the discussion on what can be learned: what worked to help calm this customer, and what might be tried differently next time. Don't make negative remarks about the customer's behavior or character. And of course, never criticize one employee in front of another.

Part Summary

In this part, you learned how to create an **environment** to foster customer satisfaction. Next, you learned how to use this book for a **staff meeting**. Finally, you learned some tips for calming **upset customers** and managing **upset employees**.

APPENDIX

Appendix to Part 3

Comments & Suggested Responses

Watch Your Words

1. This response is negative. Rephrase it as a positive response:

   "Yes, I'd be glad to hold it until closing time tonight, which is 6:00."

2. Again, this is negative. It assumes that the customer doesn't qualify. Rephrase it without the negative assumption:

   "I'd be delighted to add you to the list. This list is for customers who meet the qualification of having spent $1,000 with us this year. Does that qualification fit you?"

3. This response will make the customer feel embarrassed, and probably angry. Rephrase it to make it less personal:

   "I'm sorry for the delay. It seems that the form was not completed correctly. I'll help you put it right."

4. It doesn't answer the question. Also, it sounds like an order. Rephrase it to invite the customer to visit the Accessories Department, instead of saying he has to.

   "Yes, we do carry mittens. There's a wide selection in our Accessories Department, which is at the top of those stairs."

5. This response is not very helpful. Rephrase it to offer some assistance to the customer:

   "Let me check for you."

6. This is a flip response to a serious question. Rephrase it to give the information she asked for:

   "You can call her during her office hours, Mondays, Wednesdays, and Fridays, between 2:00 and 4:00, at 555-1212, or drop in on her during those times in Room 733, or put a note in her mailbox in Room 345. Let me write that down for you."

7. Tell the customer what you can do, not what you can't do.

   "I'm sorry, but we've closed out for the day. I'd be glad to take the information and change it first thing in the morning."

8. This is insulting to the customer, and assumes she didn't read the manual. Even if she did read the manual, she may need further clarification.

   "I'm not sure. Please tell me what it's doing and not doing and we'll troubleshoot together."

9. Not very helpful, is it? Give the information asked for:

   "Let me look that up for you. I'll be just another moment."

10. The staff person is calling the customer a liar. Rephrase it without the accusation:

    "I'm sorry for the confusion. Let me pull your record so we can see what happened and fix it. What's your last name, please?"

11. This isn't very helpful. Give the information asked for:

    "It's down this hall; take a left and you'll see it straight ahead."

12. Don't tell your customer you have other customer problems. It isn't relevant to their concern about their order, and it implies that customer problems are common in your organization. This may make them take their business elsewhere because they have lost confidence in your business. A better response is:

    "Let me look into that for you."

13. Customers don't want to hear, "It's policy." Explain how this policy is a benefit to the customer.

    "We ask for two identifications for your protection. I'm sure many other bank personnel know you, Mr. Perez. I'm new here so I want to make sure I'm not giving your money to someone who says he's you but isn't."

14. Answer the question without telling the customer what she has to do:

    "Please tell me about it and I'll see what I can do to straighten it out."

15. This is not a helpful response. It's annoying.

    "Let me walk you through it and point out the steps in the manual."

16. Never make the customer call back. It's not their problem or fault that the computer is down.

    "I'll be glad to check that for you and call you back as soon as our computer is running again."

Appendix to Part 4

Comments & Suggested Responses

Case Study: The Surly Salesperson

Let's analyze the conversation and discuss key areas of conflict.

He was blunt. The salesperson should have considered the words he used and how they can affect the customer. When the salesperson initially confronted Rebecca with "Why don't you have an 800 number?" she became annoyed. He could have said: "Congratulations on your new video, 'Calming Upset Customers.' This is Larry Smith from The Best Long Distance Telephone Company. I noticed there wasn't an 800 number listed in the announcement. I thought one would help increase your orders. Do you currently have an 800 number?"

Instead, he assumed Rebecca didn't have an 800 number. He also assumed she had placed an ad, when actually it was a press release, which meant she had no control over which information the magazine chose to publish.

When you need clarification, ask questions politely, and with sincere interest. Don't be confrontational with your questions. Modify blunt questions with, "May I ask," "Would you share with me" or "By the way."

He was argumentative. He demanded to know who in his company had misinformed Rebecca although she told him it had been over six months since she'd received the information.

If you disagree with something, don't respond with "That's not true." Instead, try, "I don't understand how that could have happened. Tell me more."

Twice he didn't listen to the answers to his questions and asked them again. Few things annoy people more than repeating answers to the same questions. If you don't remember what someone said, acknowledge it: "I'm sorry, I blanked out a moment. Would you tell me again why your 800 number isn't in this announcement?" That shows you're human and polite.

His tone of voice sounded impatient and frustrated at not making the sale. No wonder he was frustrated; because he wasn't listening to himself or Rebecca, he had no idea why he wasn't getting anywhere.

Case Study: The Annoying Airline Agents

Agent 1 didn't acknowledge Suzanne when she was done with the previous customer. She could have said pleasantly "Let me just finish this gentleman's reservation and I'll be right with you."

Agent 2 also could have acknowledged Suzanne with an "I'll be just a second" to Suzanne. When the other passenger approached him he should have said, "Let me help this woman and I'll be right with you." Or, "I'll be glad to help you with that as soon as I'm done with this customer." He helped other passengers twice before helping Suzanne, who was next in line.

Agent 1 was so busy chatting with her co-worker she didn't make sure Suzanne was going in the right direction. This leads to a potentially dangerous situation with Suzanne walking out onto the tarmac with no guidance.

The third airline employee should not have argued with Suzanne (and yes, Suzanne should not have called the other agent a twit). The third employee could have defused the situation by asking what was wrong and then escorting Suzanne to the correct door.

Case Study: The Flighty Travel Agent

The manager's responses didn't indicate a sincere attempt to help solve the problem. It didn't matter that Bianca no longer worked there. His response suggested he didn't want to take responsibility for what she had said because she was no longer an employee.

Nor did it matter how long ago the problem was noticed, as Robert had already explained the sequence of events. The manager should have focused on fixing the problem, not on inconsequential details that Robert had already covered.

The final blow was when he seemed to blame Robert for the problem by saying, "And you're just now getting around to calling about it?" Robert had been tracking the problem, and was told it would be taken care of by various employees.

Case Study: The Nervy Newsman

The salesperson was confrontational with his questions. Instead of "Why not?" a gentler question. "Really? Help me understand why," would have elicited a more informational response.

His reaction to the reason Bill wasn't resubscribing was also confrontational. "Are you kidding?" implies that Bill is a fool for not seeing the value of the paper.

Then he gets argumentative when Bill explains that he likes the business coverage in the local paper better. He's arguing with Bill's opinion. There's no possibility for a sale with this rep.

If you remember only three things, they should be:

1. Listen completely.

2. Speak respectfully.

3. Focus on positive actions.

How Would You Handle the Situation?

1. "I can understand how you'd be upset. You've waited a long time. I'll help you get through your transaction quickly. How can I help you now?"

2. "I'm sorry your account doesn't balance. Let me research your account transactions and see what went wrong so we can make sure it doesn't happen again. May I have your account number, please?"

3. "I can understand why you'd be upset. I would be too. I'm sorry your software hasn't been delivered. Let me look into what went wrong. Do you have the order number and date? Would you like to wait while I research this, or would you prefer I get back to you within the hour?"

4. "I'm sorry you are dissatisfied with my service. Please tell me specifically what wasn't right so I can correct it. And I'll get Mrs. Hall, my supervisor, for you."

5. "I can understand why you feel this procedure is a waste of time. I'm sorry, I don't have the authority to complete this transaction differently—only the manager does. When she comes back, I will check to see if I can handle your account differently next time you come in. I'm sorry for the inconvenience today."

Additional Reading

Crisp 50-Minute Series books:

Bonet, Diana. *The Business of Listening.*

Chapman, Elwood N., and Wil McKnight. *Attitude: Your Most Priceless Possession.*

Finch, Lloyd. *Telephone Courtesy and Customer Service.*

Kindler, Herbert S. *Managing Disagreement Constructively.*

Martin, William B. *Quality Customer Service.*

Minor, Marianne. *Preventing Workplace Violence.*

Other related reading:

Barlow, Janelle and Claus Moeller. *A Complaint Is a Gift.* San Francisco, CA: Berrett-Koehler, 1996.

Charles, C. Leslie. *Why Is Everyone So Cranky?* New York, NY: Hyperion, 1999.

Morgan, Rebecca L. *Life's Lessons: Insights and Information for a Richer Life.* Morgan Seminar Group, 1997.

Morgan, Rebecca L. *Grow Your Key Talent: Thought-Provoking Essays for Business Owners, Executives and Managers on Developing Star Staff.* Morgan Seminar Group, 2009.

Morgan, Rebecca L. *Remarkable Customer Service… and Disservice: Case Studies and Discussions to Increase Your Customers' Delight.* Morgan Seminar Group, 2009.

Stiel, Holly. *Thank You Very Much: A Book for Anyone Who Has Ever Said, "May I help you?"* Berkeley, CA: Ten Speed Press, 1995.

Zemke, Ron, and John Woods, eds. *Best Practices in Customer Service.* New York, NY: AMACOM, 1999.